SCOTLAND*on*SUNDAY

KU-629-864

PUB QUIZ

Collins

HarperCollins Publishers
Westerhill Road, Bishopbriggs
Glasgow G64 2QT

The Collins website is www.collins.co.uk

This edition produced especially for *Scotland on Sunday*

© HarperCollinsPublishers 2005

ISBN 0 00 776060-4

Printed and bound in Great Britain by
Clays Ltd, St Ives plc

HOW TO USE THIS BOOK

Collins Pub Quiz is simply designed and easy to use.

QUESTIONS

Each of the pages has a set of questions covering aspects of popular knowledge and culture. Ten of the questions fall into specific categories, while the eleventh in each set, the 'True or False?' question, can be used either as a tie-breaker or just as a regular question.

ANSWERS

The answers page-number for each set is flagged at the foot of its questions page. In some answers, especially in the 'True or False?' category, part of the answer appears in brackets. This is simply given as extra information and is not essential to answer the question correctly – although you can use it that way, if you want to give your quiz a harder edge.

Have fun with the questions, and good luck!

Food & Drink
What did Snow White's wicked stepmother use to tempt her?

Natural World
Loch Garten is famous for which bird of prey?

History
How many of Henry VIII's wives lost their heads?

Culture & Belief
If a god was Cupid in Rome, what could he expect to be called in Greece?

Stage & Screen
How many different centuries did Edmund Blackadder appear in?

Written Word
In what town did Roy of the Rovers play football?

Music
On what road did Nellie the Elephant meet the head of the herd?

Famous People
The 1956 marriage of what two seeming opposites prompted the headline 'Egghead marries Hourglass'?

Sport & Leisure
Why would you be given a green jacket and a yellow jersey?

Science & Tech
What world-renowned scientist played himself in an episode of *Star Trek: The Next Generation*?

True or False?
The American inventor of the deep-freezing process was a Mr Birdseye; true or false?

ANSWERS: PAGE 82

Food & Drink — What did the Israelites eat in the desert?

Natural World — How high is an equine hand?

History — What Roman Emperor made his horse a senator?

Culture & Belief — Whose New Look caused a sensation in post-war fashion?

Stage & Screen — The folk tune *Johnny Todd* was the theme music to what ground-breaking British cop drama of the 1960s?

Written Word — What classic English work of literature features The Summoner, The Man Of Law and The Wife Of Bath?

Music — Whose *Song of Joy* is the anthem of the European Union?

Famous People — What famous sleuth contracted gangrene from biting his tongue after stumbling on an uneven pavement?

Sport & Leisure — In what town do Raith Rovers play?

Science & Tech — What famous motor manufacturer invented the motor car?

True or False? — Sideburns were named after a prominent wearer, US Civil War General Ambrose E. Burnside; true or false?

ANSWERS: PAGE 82

The berries of what shrub-like plant are used to make gin?

 What is the Windy City?

 Why did the royal family move from Saxe-Coburg to Windsor?

 Where did Panama hats originate?

 In the climax of what film does the male lead climb down the presidential faces at Mount Rushmore?

 Who wrote *Look Back In Anger*?

 Who wrote *Don't Look Back In Anger*?

 Whose journeys aboard *The Beagle* allowed some revolutionary theories to evolve?

 What BBC TV programme popularised snooker as a spectator sport?

 Where would you find a Plimsoll Line?

 Scotland Yard was originally the name of a medieval house used by Scots kings visiting London; true or false?

ANSWERS: PAGE 82

Food & Drink What is Port Salut?

 Natural World What is the aurora borealis also known as?

 History How many Elizabeths reigned as queen in Scotland before Elizabeth II?

 Culture & Belief What God-given gift did Moses receive at Mount Sinai?

 Stage & Screen Who played Moses in the 1956 film *The Ten Commandments*?

 Written Word What Irish politician wrote a spy novel called *The Riddle Of The Sands*?

 Music What are 'Hammersmith Palais, the Bolshoi Ballet, jump back in the alley and nanny goats'?

 Famous People What business, apart from the movies, did Howard Hughes make his millions in?

 Sport & Leisure What was the official name of the original World Cup?

 Science & Tech What was the first British jet airliner?

 True or False? The first non-white British MP was elected over 100 years ago; true or false?

ANSWERS: PAGE 82

Food & Drink — What classic ad featured an alien family laughing at a traditional Earth recipe?

 Natural World — If the northern lights are the aurora borealis, what are the southern lights called?

 History — How many amendments have there been to the US Constitution?

 Culture & Belief — What would a Scotsman tell an Englishman to do with a quaich?

 Stage & Screen — What is Bollywood?

 Written Word — What miser lost his gold but found a treasure in his adopted child?

 Music — Whose daughter was *My Darling Clementine*?

 Famous People — What did Oscar Wilde consider to be the curse of the drinking classes?

 Sport & Leisure — In what year did Mark Spitz win several Olympic swimming golds?

 Science & Tech — What explosive device was invented by Alfred B. Nobel, founder of the Nobel Peace Prize?

 True or False? — The Queen holds UK passport number 1; true or false?

ANSWERS: PAGE 82

Food & Drink What is the ingredient which turns curry yellow?

 Natural World What natural feature is common to Tanzania, Uganda, Sudan and Egypt?

 History Who was killed on the Ides of March?

 Culture & Belief What date is the Ides of March?

 Stage & Screen Whose undersea world was visited by *Calypso*?

 Written Word Who did Hamlet tell to get to a nunnery?

 Music What two 1950s pop stars died in the same plane crash as Buddy Holly?

 Famous People What famous divorcée once declared 'One can never be too rich or too thin'?

 Sport & Leisure In what events did Jesse Owens win his four gold medals in the 1936 Berlin Olympics?

 Science & Tech Name the Scottish vet who invented the pneumatic tyre?

 True or False? More people were killed in the 1906 San Francisco earthquake than on the *Titanic* in 1912; true or false?

ANSWERS: PAGE 83

Food & Drink — If it's heavy in Scotland, what is it in England?

 Natural World — What is catgut traditionally made from?

 History — Who foresaw his country's civil war in the phrase 'A house divided against itself cannot stand'?

 Culture & Belief — What is bogyphobia a fear of?

 Stage & Screen — Name three of the Tracey brothers from *Thunderbirds*.

 Written Word — What was the name of Sherlock Holmes' smarter brother?

 Music — What song opened the first live broadcast of Radio 1 in 1967?

 Famous People — How did Mahatma Gandhi, Indira Gandhi and Rajiv Gandhi die?

 Sport & Leisure — Where is kabbadi most frequently played?

 Science & Tech — What British classic first went on sale in 1959 costing £496 19s 2d?

 True or False? — A granny, a sheepshank and a bowline are all parts of a chimney; true or false?

ANSWERS: PAGE 83

Food & Drink
What do you get if you boil sheep's offal, oats, suet and spices in a sheep's stomach bag?

 Natural World
What deer is not actually a deer but a member of the caribou family?

 History
What year saw slavery officially ended in the USA, to within five years?

 Culture & Belief
What European head of state wears a crown but is not a monarch?

 Stage & Screen
Who starred in a biopic of US husband-and-wife dance team Vernon and Irene Castle?

 Written Word
Whose seductive dance before King Herod was rewarded with the head of John the Baptist?

 Music
What American state is the home of country-and-western music?

 Famous People
What did Leonardo da Vinci, Jack the Ripper and Horatio Nelson have in common?

 Sport & Leisure
What are the chances of throwing a double-six with two dice?

 Science & Tech
What is the seventh planet from the Sun?

 True or False?
There are six counties in the province of Ulster; true or false?

ANSWERS: PAGE 83

Food & Drink
What two foods originate in the Italian town of Parma?

 Natural World
What is a shooting star?

 History
What, founded in 330 BC, was the world's first state-funded scientific institution?

 Culture & Belief
How much money would you gamble if you bet a brace of ponies?

 Stage & Screen
What four-legged companion went with Dorothy from Kansas to Oz?

 Written Word
If the *Times* came from London and the *Herald* from Glasgow, where did the *Guardian* come from?

 Music
'Satchmo' was the nickname of what jazz legend?

 Famous People
What is the name 'Satchmo' short for?

 Sport & Leisure
Who said in 1966, 'They think it's all over – it is now'?

 Science & Tech
How did Valentina Tereshkova shoot to fame in 1963?

 True or False?
James VI of Scotland and I of England wrote an anti-smoking tract in 1604; true or false?

ANSWERS: PAGE 83

Food & Drink What is the Greek pastry baklava sweetened with?

 Natural World What is the world's second-highest mountain?

 History What happened at 11:00 a.m. on 11 November, 1918?

 Culture & Belief How many years would you be married if you were celebrating your tin wedding anniversary?

 Stage & Screen Whose screen test reported 'Can't act, can't sing, slightly bald. Can dance a little'?

 Written Word Who was Graham Greene's *Third Man*?

 Music What was the opening song of the Live Aid concert at Wembley Stadium in July 1985?

 Famous People Whose 1938 radio production of *War of The Worlds* had thousands of Americans fleeing invading Martians?

 Sport & Leisure Who won football's first World Cup?

 Science & Tech What US politician was the first American to orbit the Earth?

 True or False? Bagpipers run the risk of lung infections from bacteria which lurk inside their bags; true or false?

ANSWERS: PAGE 83

What is the main ingredient in Palestine soup?

 What are Bailey, Malin and German Bight?

 What scholarly monarch was called 'the wisest fool in Christendom'?

 What does 'amen' mean?

 Who had a *Brief Encounter*?

 Who created *The Simpsons*?

 What famous Irish folk band did James Galway and Van Morrison record hit albums with?

 Where was Thomas à Becket murdered?

 What board game, invented in 1931, was first called Criss-Cross?

 How long, to the nearest minute, does sunlight take to reach the Earth?

 Adolf Hitler used his grandmother's name of Schicklgruber for several years; true or false?

ANSWERS: PAGE 84

Food & Drink What drink taught the world to sing in the 1970s?

 Natural World What is the capital of Australia?

 History Which side fired the first shot in the American Civil War?

 Culture & Belief What was the only thing that remained in Pandora's Box?

 Stage & Screen What cult 1980s film had *Man In Motion* by John Parr as its theme?

 Written Word What was Superman's original home town called?

 Music What is the term for a group of seven performing musicians?

 Famous People Who was the original millionaire philanthropist who built and owned Skibo Castle in Sutherland?

 Sport & Leisure In which sport would you encounter a jerk?

 Science & Tech What is deoxyribonucleic acid better known as?

 True or False? Margaret Thatcher was a member of the Labour Party for almost two years in her youth; true or false?

ANSWERS: PAGE 84

What would you find in the middle of a Sussex Pond Pudding?

 What is the world's largest island (excluding the continents)?

 How many Jameses were kings of Scots?

 What date was Jesus conceived on?

 What 1960s children's TV show featured Vienna's Lippizaner horses?

 Who is Eric Blair better known as?

 What did Judy Collins have in common with the Royal Scots Dragoon Guards?

 What European leader used his presidential powers to check a takeover of his favourite brewery?

 Which two teams met in the world's first international football fixture?

 What elementary discovery was made by Crick and Watson?

 Sumer is Icumen In, from the 13th century, is the earliest known musical canon; true or false?

ANSWERS: PAGE 84

Food & Drink
What drink is known as uisge beatha (pronounced 'ooskay baa'), meaning the water of life?

Natural World
What country uses the zloty as currency?

History
What event was the Crystal Palace built to house?

Culture & Belief
What church recruits unwitting followers through posthumous baptism ceremonies?

Stage & Screen
What town is Coronation Street in?

Written Word
What writer turned down a peerage and the Order of Merit but accepted the Nobel Prize for Literature?

Music
Who urged his listeners to *Keep Right On To The End Of The Road*?

Famous People
Who was the second man to walk on the moon?

Sport & Leisure
Who was Britain's first million-pound footballer?

Science & Tech
What do the saxophone, the guillotine and the biro pen have in common?

True or False?
Until the 19th century, Italian boy sopranos could be castrated to preserve their high voices; true or false?

ANSWERS: PAGE 84

Food & Drink
What is the vegetable Americans call an eggplant known as in Britain?

 Natural World
What makes a humming bird hum?

 History
Who was the second Lord Protector of England, Scotland and Ireland?

 Culture & Belief
What religion reveres the god Krishna?

 Stage & Screen
What was the name of Powell and Pressburger's film production company?

 Written Word
Who did Gore Vidal call 'the Acting President'?

 Music
What conductor got classical music in Birmingham all shook up?

 Famous People
What politician was called 'the Uncrowned King of Ireland'?

 Sport & Leisure
At which Olympics did synchronised swimming first appear?

 Science & Tech
What is iron oxide more commonly known as?

 True or False?
English is the world's most-spoken language; true or false?

ANSWERS: PAGE 84

Food & Drink What is scampi made from?

 Natural World What city was previously known as Byzantium and Constantinople?

 History Who were 'overpaid, oversexed and over here'?

 Culture & Belief What Israeli king did both Donatello and Michelangelo sculpt?

 Stage & Screen What two antipodean wonders spoke in a language humans could understand?

 Written Word What is the name of Dennis the Menace's dog?

 Music What kilted singer asked *Donald, Where's Yer Troosers*?

 Famous People Who declared 'I can resist everything except temptation'?

 Sport & Leisure What city hosted the first Olympic Games of the modern era?

 Science & Tech What would you be studying if your subject was virology?

 True or False? Orson Welles and Rita Hayworth were husband and wife; true or false?

ANSWERS: PAGE 85

Food & Drink Whose divine dinners consisted of ambrosia and nectar?

 Natural World What country is Kathmandu the capital of?

 History What was the last battle fought on British soil?

 Culture & Belief Whose 1920s' ad campaign permanently changed Father Christmas' costume from green to red?

 Stage & Screen Who wrote *A Streetcar Named Desire*?

 Written Word What recollections make up the world's longest novel?

 Music What top British band used to be known as Seymour?

 Famous People What evangelical preacher supported Richard Nixon and prayed at Bill Clinton's inauguration?

 Sport & Leisure How many balls are on a snooker table at the start of a game?

 Science & Tech How many teeth does the adult human have?

 True or False? By 1996, Britain's favourite food was still fish and chips; true or false?

ANSWERS: PAGE 85

Food & Drink What guerrilla fighter had a biscuit named after him?

 Natural World If you had panophobia, what would you fear?

 History What was the last state to join the American Union?

 Culture & Belief How many languages are allowed by law to be used in adverts in France?

 Stage & Screen Who do Father Dougal and Father Jack share the Craggy Island parochial house with?

 Written Word The novels of what Edinburgh writer were used to name a football team and a railway station?

 Music What Kenny Rogers song sparked a series of four TV movies?

 Famous People What head of state did the American CIA reputedly try to assassinate with an exploding cigar?

 Sport & Leisure Who was the first player to win the Wimbledon Men's Championship five times in a row?

 Science & Tech What fraction is used to express pi?

 True or False? An antimacassar was a special kind of mop used to polish Victorian tiled floors; true or false?

ANSWERS: PAGE 85

Food & Drink
What ballerina gave her name to an Australian pudding?

 Natural World
How far would you have to journey to get to the centre of the Earth?

 History
Who is the First Lord of the Treasury?

 Culture & Belief
What New York State farm gave its name to a landmark event of the flower-power era in 1969?

 Stage & Screen
What FBI duo believe The Truth is Out There?

 Written Word
What cartoon strip, inspiring a TV sitcom and movie, was created by Charles Addams?

 Music
What would a bagpiper do with a chanter?

 Famous People
Who was the Young Pretender?

 Sport & Leisure
What sport developed from the first Hawaii Ironman Competition in 1974?

 Science & Tech
Until 1745, what were barbers officially able to perform as well as haircuts?

True or False?
The pound note first came into circulation during the Napoleonic Wars; true or false?

ANSWERS: PAGE 85

Food & Drink What was John the Baptist said to have eaten in the desert?

 Natural World Arches, loops, whorls and composites are all types of what?

 History How many members were originally in the Common Market?

 Culture & Belief What saint prayed, 'Oh Lord, make me chaste, but not yet?'

 Stage & Screen What grumpy pensioner had *One Foot in the Grave*?

 Written Word What science fiction author wrote the *Earthsea* trilogy?

 Music What band topped the UK chart in 1996 with *Spaceman*?

 Famous People Whose granddaughter Patti was kidnapped by the Symbionese Liberation Army?

 Sport & Leisure In which sport would you find soling, Flying Dutchman and tornado competition classes?

 Science & Tech What temperature does water boil at on the Fahrenheit scale?

 True or False? A sponge is an animal; true or false?

ANSWERS: PAGE 85

Mashed neeps and tatties are the traditional accompaniments to what Scots delicacy?

 How many time zones are there in mainland USA?

 What were the colours of the first two British stamps?

 What American terrorist group took their name from a line in a Bob Dylan song?

 What does *ER* stand for?

 What novel, by a former teacher, charts the descent into savagery of boys marooned on a desert island?

 What band sang about *Waterloo Sunset*?

 What Argentinian doctor was boss of Cuba's national bank before going to Bolivia to start a revolution?

 Where was netball invented?

 If you suffered from hypotension would your blood pressure be too high or too low?

 Patagonia is a fictitious land from the works of 18th-century satirist Jonathan Swift; true or false?

ANSWERS: PAGE 86

Food & Drink — What is the minimum age for a malt whisky?

 Natural World — What does a limnologist study?

 History — What was William the Bastard's more common nickname?

 Culture & Belief — What would a yachtsman use a burgee for?

 Stage & Screen — What was odd about the TV detective pairing of Randall and Hopkirk?

 Written Word — Where did Kubla Khan a stately pleasure-dome decree?

 Music — Who wrote the opera *Madame Butterfly*?

 Famous People — What British leader was described as 'a very big woman, terrifying to look at, with a fierce look'?

 Sport & Leisure — Which three of the five Classic horse races make up the English Triple Crown?

 Science & Tech — What is the only organ in the human body capable of regeneration?

 True or False? — A Mr Fahrenheit invented the mercury thermometer; true or false?

ANSWERS: PAGE 86

Food & Drink What Biblical character spent three days and nights as fish food?

 Natural World What American state is Juneau the capital of?

 History Who was the USA's first Catholic president?

 Culture & Belief What two brothers with a talent for promotion coined the phrase 'Labour Isn't Working' in 1978?

 Stage & Screen Who did King Kong fall for in the 1933 movie?

 Written Word What was the significance of *Fahrenheit 451*?

 Music What chart-topping duo did Vince Clark form after he left Yazoo?

 Famous People What US president's previous jobs included that of male model?

 Sport & Leisure Which is the fastest of all ball games?

 Science & Tech How many degrees' difference is there between 0° Centigrade and 0° Kelvin, to the nearest 10°?

 True or False? Allan Pinkerton, founder of the famous American detective agency, was a Glaswegian; true or false?

ANSWERS: PAGE 86

Food & Drink
What, according to Dr Johnson, was eaten by horses in England and people in Scotland?

Natural World
What is the world's highest waterfall?

History
Which Robert do Bobbies take their name from?

Culture & Belief
What would an American keep in his billfold?

Stage & Screen
What is the family relationship between Francis Ford Coppola and Nicholas Cage?

Written Word
Who wrote *The Godfather*?

Music
What in the First World War went ting-a-ling-a-ling for you but not for me?

Famous People
Who was T. E. Lawrence better known as?

Sport & Leisure
What is the exact imperial distance of a marathon race?

Science & Tech
What size are the internal angles of an equilateral triangle?

True or False?
Water drains down plugholes clockwise in the Southern Hemisphere; true or false?

ANSWERS: PAGE 86

Food & Drink
What, until the BSE scare, was Desperate Dan's favourite food?

Natural World
What mammal's pregnancies last longer than any other on earth?

History
What do the initials 'G.I.' stand for?

Culture & Belief
What saint is represented by the emblem of a shower of rain?

Stage & Screen
What classic British wartime drama won two Oscars for its star and creator, Noël Coward?

Written Word
What writer said 'Other people have a nationality. The Irish and the Jews have a psychosis'?

Music
What is an aria in an opera?

Famous People
What fashion designer first came to prominence with her bondage wear during the punk era?

Sport & Leisure
What weapon is used in the Japanese martial art of kendo?

Science & Tech
Why is ethylene glycol added to car engines?

True or False?
Scotch whisky is also produced in Japan; true or false?

ANSWERS: PAGE 86

Food & Drink
In what decade did sliced bread first appear?

 Natural World
What causes the tides?

 History
What fleet-footed IRA kidnap victim from the 1980s was never seen again?

 Culture & Belief
Which of the 12 apostles was the tax-collector?

 Stage & Screen
What film had *Moon River* as its theme music?

 Written Word
What cartoon-strip family comprises Homer, Marge, Lisa, Bart and Maggie?

 Music
Who were *Pretty Vacant* in 1977?

 Famous People
What two historic martial heroes guard the gateway to Edinburgh Castle?

 Sport & Leisure
How many fences are there in the Aintree Grand National?

 Science & Tech
How many ounces are there in a kilogram, approximately?

 True or False?
Kr is the symbol used to represent the element Krypton in the Periodic Table; true or false?

ANSWERS: PAGE 87

Food & Drink
What biscuit did West Country physician Dr William Oliver give his name to?

Natural World
How much skin is on the average adult male body, to the nearest square foot?

History
When was the United Kingdom founded?

Culture & Belief
What did the East End Revival Society become in 1878?

Stage & Screen
Who made the films *Gregory's Girl* and *Local Hero*?

Written Word
Who is credited with writing *The Iliad* and *The Odyssey*?

Music
What famous West End musical is based on a collection of children's poems by T. S. Eliot?

Famous People
What utilitarian philosopher espoused the greatest happiness for the greatest number?

Sport & Leisure
Which US city plays host to the world's oldest annual marathon?

Science & Tech
How many litres of air does a fit adult take in with each breath?

True or False?
The lawnmower was invented by a Mr Budding; true or false?

ANSWERS: PAGE 87

Food & Drink What prime minister's last words were 'I think I could eat one of Bellamy's veal pies'?

 Natural World How many countries are there in Great Britain?

 History What three Queens had Glasgow as their first home town?

 Culture & Belief What item of fashion did Mary Quant invent?

 Stage & Screen What military rank did James Bond hold?

 Written Word Who wrote *Ulysses*?

 Music Whose album *Arrival* topped the UK charts in 1977?

 Famous People Who was manager of Manchester United at the time of the Munich Air Disaster?

 Sport & Leisure Which is the oldest of the English Classic horse races?

 Science & Tech What does vulcanisation do to rubber?

 True or False? New York boasted the world's first skyscraper; true or false?

ANSWERS: PAGE 87

Food & Drink What is Mulligatawny?

 Natural World What group of individuals swear their ethical fitness in the Hippocratic Oath?

 History What street did the Great Fire of London start in?

 Culture & Belief Before 1752, on what date did the year begin in Britain?

 Stage & Screen What three films have each won 11 Oscars?

 Written Word What was the name of Don Quixote's sidekick?

 Music What are 'whiskers on kittens, bright copper kettles and warm woollen mittens'?

 Famous People Rockers Richie Sambora and Tommy Lee have both married which beautiful blonde?

 Sport & Leisure How many times did Jackie Stewart win the Formula One World Drivers' Championship?

 Science & Tech What does the Mohs scale measure?

 True or False? Humans have more body hairs than apes; true or false?

ANSWERS: PAGE 87

Food & Drink   What drink did the British in India take as an anti-malarial?

 Natural World   What bird has the largest wingspan?

 History   What famous World War One field marshal drowned off the north of Scotland in 1915?

 Culture & Belief   How long does Passover last?

 Stage & Screen   What unlikely POW movie featured Max von Sydow, Bobby Moore, Sylvester Stallone and John Wark?

 Written Word   What story was inspired by the sinking of the whisky-laden *SS Politician* in 1941?

 Music   Who had a UK top 10 hit in 1967 with a version of *Eidelweiss*?

 Famous People   Whose mammoth movie career ended in a sex-and murder scandal in 1921?

 Sport & Leisure   Who was the last winner of BBC TV's *Pot Black* snooker championship in 1986?

 Science & Tech   What is a polygraph used to detect?

 True or False?   Louis Braille, inventor of readable type for the blind, was not blind himself; true or false?

ANSWERS: PAGE 87

What is the difference between whisky and whiskey?

 What is the fastest bird in the world?

 What war was income tax first introduced to finance?

 What Christian feast is celebrated on Whit Sunday?

 In what film would you find Sean Thornton, Mary Kate Danaher and Michaeleen Oge Flynn?

 What two books did Robert Louis Stevenson's hero David Balfour appear in?

 According to the song, what will we do 'though cowards flinch and traitors sneer'?

 What music producer was famous for his 'wall of sound' production techniques?

 Who was the first cricketer officially to be recorded hitting a six off each ball in a six-ball over?

 How many carats are there in pure gold?

 Vulcanised rubber was invented by a Mr Pirelli; true or false?

ANSWERS: PAGE 88

Food & Drink
How many pints of beer are in a hogshead?

Natural World
What is known as the Staff of Life?

History
What Englishman was described as 'The Hammer of the Scots'?

Culture & Belief
How many rooms, to the nearest hundred, are in the world's largest palace in Brunei?

Stage & Screen
Where in London did the Wombles live?

Written Word
Sinbad, Aladdin and Ali Baba all originally appeared in what volume?

Music
What is the libretto of an opera?

Famous People
Who is singer-songwriter Declan McManus better known as?

Sport & Leisure
In which Far Eastern country did the martial art of Taekwondo originate?

Science & Tech
How much would a ten-stone man weigh on Jupiter?

True or False?
Ernest Hemingway co-wrote the screenplay of the 1946 version of *The Big Sleep*; true or false?

ANSWERS: PAGE 88

Food & Drink
What notorious gambler invented an easy-to-eat snack so he would not have to leave his card table?

Natural World
What seas are linked by the Kiel Canal?

History
What was the fate of the Stone of Destiny at Christmas, 1950?

Culture & Belief
What colour does a Sikh bride wear on her wedding day?

Stage & Screen
What Hitchcock film shows its action entirely from the viewpoint of a house-bound photographer?

Written Word
What craft did Madame Defarge perfect in Charles Dickens' *A Tale Of Two Cities*?

Music
What two singers had hits with *I Will Always Love You*?

Famous People
Wagner's most famous fan was a politician who often played his music at rallies; who was he?

Sport & Leisure
What four titles comprise tennis' Grand Slam?

Science & Tech
Where would you expect to find a convection current?

True or False?
Ho Chi Minh was told that he could become the world's greatest pastry chef if he gave up politics; true or false?

ANSWERS: PAGE 88

Food & Drink
What is the traditional fare on Shrove Tuesday?

 Natural World
What is the lowest area on the Earth's surface?

 History
In what century were the first Olympic Games held in Greece?

 Culture & Belief
What is the term for a painting done on a freshly plastered wall?

 Stage & Screen
What does a best boy do on a film crew?

 Written Word
Whose ghost haunted *Macbeth*?

 Music
What US presidential candidate used Fleetwood Mac's *Don't Stop* as his campaign theme?

 Famous People
By what title is the Earl of Inverness and Baron Killyleagh better known?

 Sport & Leisure
What sport began in Holland, was later popularised in Scotland then dominated by Canada in modern times?

 Science & Tech
What might you see if refraction occurred during precipitation?

 True or False?
An 'oxbow' is the name of a type of knot; true or false?

ANSWERS: PAGE 88

Food & Drink What drink is made from molasses?

 Natural World Where is the Great Barrier Reef?

 History What was the official title of the Poll Tax?

 Culture & Belief What design style did the 1925 Exposition des Arts Décoratifs in Paris give rise to?

 Stage & Screen Who promised 'I'll be back'?

 Written Word Who was the deformed sexton in Victor Hugo's *Notre Dame De Paris*?

 Music Who wrote *The Mighty Quinn*?

 Famous People Who was the last Hanoverian monarch of Britain?

 Sport & Leisure Greco-Roman and Freestyle are the two main types of which sport?

 Science & Tech What is a CAT scanner generally used to find?

 True or False? Buffalo Bill once kicked off a football match at Glasgow's Hampden Park; true or false?

ANSWERS: PAGE 88

Food & Drink What did Jesus do at the Cana wedding feast?

 Natural World How many chromosomes are in a normal human body cell?

 History What Prime Minister gave Britain the three-day week?

 Culture & Belief What do American babies wear on their bottoms?

 Stage & Screen Name two of the three films which have won Oscars for animator Nick Parks.

 Written Word What was the name of Bertie Wooster's club?

 Music Who, according to Robert Burns' song, did the deil, or devil, dance away with?

 Famous People What small item is Alec Issigonis famous for designing?

 Sport & Leisure How many players does a Gaelic Football team have?

 Science & Tech What recurrent stellar visitor to Earth was featured on the Bayeux Tapestry?

 True or False? The Morris Mini was the first British car to sell one million; true or false?

ANSWERS: PAGE 89

Food & Drink What red meat has the lowest fat content?

Natural World What animal's name means 'river horse'?

History What was the relationship between Indian prime ministers Jawaharlal Nehru and Indira Gandhi?

Culture & Belief Where can the Wallace Monument be found?

Stage & Screen Who played Dr Kildare in the long-running 1960s TV series?

Written Word What million-selling book caused Alexander Solzhenitsyn's deportation from the USSR in 1973?

Music What Viennese father and son were renowned masters of the waltz?

Famous People What did the 'F' in JFK stand for?

Sport & Leisure What is the highest possible judo grade?

Science & Tech What man-made vehicle holds the all-time speed record?

True or False? Nitrogen is the second-biggest component of the air we breathe; true or false?

ANSWERS: PAGE 89

Food & Drink — Which contains more caffeine – coffee beans or tea leaves?

 Natural World — What period of Earth's history came first – Jurassic or Carboniferous?

 History — What are the Tower of London's Yeomen of the Guard better known as?

 Culture & Belief — What was St Paul's trade?

 Stage & Screen — What *Dallas* regular first made his name playing opposite a genie in *I Dream of Jeannie*?

 Written Word — How did James Joyce immortalise 16th June 1904, the day he first 'walked out' with his future wife, Nora?

 Music — What song originally by Lord Rockingham's XI, was used in a wine-gums commercial in the mid 1990s?

 Famous People — Who is fourth in line to the British throne?

 Sport & Leisure — Who is the most-capped Scottish footballer?

 Science & Tech — What Apollo space mission put the first men on the Moon?

 True or False? — Sir Walter Raleigh invented an early form of the bicycle; true or false?

ANSWERS: PAGE 89

Food & Drink — Which are generally hotter – green or red chillis?

 Natural World — What function does the human appendix perform?

 History — What political party introduced the old-age pension?

 Culture & Belief — Who dreamt of a ladder, changed his name and fathered 12 children to lead Israel's 12 tribes?

 Stage & Screen — What 1970s US drama featured a family living through the Depression in Virginia's Blue Ridge Mountains?

 Written Word — What did the famous Sun headline 'Gotcha' refer to?

 Music — According to the song, what did I spy on the streets of Laredo?

 Famous People — What politician's criticisms were likened to being savaged by a dead sheep?

 Sport & Leisure — In what sport is the Camanachd Cup the premier competition?

 Science & Tech — If oxygen is O_2, what is O_3?

 True or False? — Queen Victoria was the first European monarch to use a telephone; true or false?

ANSWERS: PAGE 89

Food & Drink
What spirit is made from potatoes?

Natural World
What is the biggest lake in Britain?

History
Who were Churchill's Few?

Culture & Belief
What Chinese philosopher was so revered he was worshipped as a god?

Stage & Screen
Which famous 1960s pop star provided the TV voice of *Thomas the Tank Engine*?

Written Word
Who wrote *The First Blast Of The Trumpet Against The Monstrous Regiment Of Women*?

Music
Where was the Tamla Motown record company first established?

Famous People
Why did Rolls-Royce change their car's badge colour from red to black?

Sport & Leisure
What tournament was thought up in 1955 by Gabriel Hanot, soccer editor of French newspaper *L'Equipe*?

Science & Tech
What road-safety device was invented by Percy Shaw in 1934?

True or False?
The Caesarean section operation was named after Julius Caesar who was thought to have been born that way; true or false?

ANSWERS: PAGE 89

Food & Drink — What is glorious about August 12th?

Natural World — How many capitals does South Africa have?

History — In what country did the sauna originate?

Culture & Belief — What three saints' crosses are represented on the Union Flag?

Stage & Screen — What were the names of the Flowerpot Men?

Written Word — Where did Professor Moriarty meet his death at the hands of Sherlock Holmes?

Music — What member of *Monty Python's Flying Circus* provided the theme song for *One Foot In The Grave*?

Famous People — Who led the famous Dambusters raid during the Second World War?

Sport & Leisure — What Scottish pastime did Hugh Munro give his name to?

Science & Tech — Where would you find a lancet, a galilee and a finial?

True or False? — The tibia bone's connected to the radius bone; true or false?

ANSWERS: PAGE 90

Food & Drink
To what profession of Frenchman would you give a *pourboire* (literally meaning 'for drinking')?

Natural World
In which Scottish region would you find John O' Groats?

History
Which country was Montezuma ruler of?

Culture & Belief
What is Montezuma's Revenge?

Stage & Screen
Who played *The Blues Brothers*?

Written Word
Whose political views were set out in the book entitled *My Struggle*?

Music
Who was *Kissing With Confidence* in 1983?

Famous People
What famous model of the 1960s was known as The Shrimp?

Sport & Leisure
Who missed the penalty that put England out of the 1996 European Championships?

Science & Tech
How many ounces to the pound are there in the troy system?

True or False?
A carillon is the specific name given to a chorister in Canterbury Cathedral; true or false?

ANSWERS: PAGE 90

Food & Drink How many lumps of sugar are in a can of non-diet fizzy drink?

Natural World Which sex of elephants have tusks – male or female?

History What addition was once made to army uniforms to stop soldiers wiping their noses on their sleeves?

Culture & Belief Which church's great bell is the largest in the UK?

Stage & Screen How much were actress Betty Grable's renowned 'million dollar legs' actually insured for?

Written Word Which Victorian detective described his toughest cases as 'three-pipe problems'?

Music Which of the three Bee Gees was the youngest?

Famous People Louis Farrakhan is a leader of which organisation?

Sport & Leisure Which animal appears on the badges of both Dumbarton FC and Coventry FC?

Science & Tech What are the three primary colours for artists?

True or False? Legendary sleuth Sherlock Holmes played the saxophone; true or false?

ANSWERS: PAGE 90

Food & Drink What type of dish is bouillabaisse?

 Natural World What part of the eye determines its colour?

 History How many pre-decimal pennies was a florin worth?

 Culture & Belief What, according to the proverb, do listeners never hear?

 Stage & Screen What film features a central scene at the top of the big wheel in a deserted Viennese funfair?

 Written Word In the story *The Three Billy Goats Gruff*, what fearsome creature was hiding under the bridge?

 Music In the song *Jailhouse Rock*, what did the warder tell Sad Sack to use instead of a partner?

 Famous People What publishing tycoon's life was reputedly the inspiration for the film *Citizen Kane*?

 Sport & Leisure How many Formula 1 races had Mika Hakkinen won before the 1998 Grand Prix race season?

 Science & Tech How tall, to the nearest 10 ft, is London's St Paul's Cathedral?

 True or False? Jackie Stewart won more grand prix races than Nigel Mansell; true or false?

Food & Drink
What kind of sauce is the basis for tartare sauce?

 Natural World
A liger is a cross between which two animals?

 History
How many decimal pennies was a florin worth at the time of decimalisation?

 Culture & Belief
When poverty comes in at the door, what does the proverb say flies out of the window?

 Stage & Screen
Who was Diana Rigg's predecessor as John Steed's sidekick in *The Avengers*?

 Written Word
What is the name of the little boy in the *Winnie-the-Pooh* stories?

 Music
What band was Louise a member of before leaving to go solo?

 Famous People
Who was noted for his stylised illustrations for Oscar Wilde's *Salome*?

 Sport & Leisure
Who were the second Scottish football team to win nine successive league championships?

 Science & Tech
What type of bridge construction is the Forth Rail Bridge?

 True or False?
The MGM lion is named Leo; true or false?

ANSWERS: PAGE 90

Food & Drink
What colour are pistachio nuts?

 Natural World
What group of islands does Fair Isle belong to?

 History
What well-loved British institution clocked up its half-century in 1998?

 Culture & Belief
What event are hot cross buns supposed to commemorate?

 Stage & Screen
Who played the part of Fagin in the 1968 film *Oliver!*?

 Written Word
What legendary film reviewer said '*Frankenstein* and *My Fair Lady* are really the same story'?

 Music
Who is Paul McCartney's musician brother?

 Famous People
Who was the Queen's unexpected companion in her bedchamber in July 1982?

 Sport & Leisure
Ice hockey is the national sport of what country?

 Science & Tech
Which textile is only genuine if handwoven in the Outer Hebrides?

 True or False?
The Shetland pony is the smallest breed of horse; true or false?

ANSWERS: PAGE 91

Food & Drink
Which ingredient in some toothpastes is also used to make scones rise?

Natural World
How many teeth does an adult human have?

History
What was special about the sailing of the ship *Empire Windrush* to Britain in 1948?

Culture & Belief
What festival is celebrated three days after Maundy Thursday?

Stage & Screen
What type of product was featured on the first TV commercial?

Written Word
What pirate had a parrot that cried 'Pieces of eight! Pieces of eight!'?

Music
What wacky 1960s band featured both Mike McGear and poet Roger McGough?

Famous People
Which Pacific island eventually became home to Scottish author Robert Louis Stevenson?

Sport & Leisure
When was the Wimbledon Tennis Championship opened to professionals?

Science & Tech
How many funnels did the *Titanic* have?

True or False?
If your diet consisted only of rabbit meat, you would die of vitamin deficiency; true or false?

Food & Drink — What American town is the home of Coca-Cola?

Natural World — What holiday islands' former name translates as The Fortunate Islands?

History — Which Scottish king killed Duncan and was himself killed by Duncan's son Malcolm?

Culture & Belief — In what country have half a million Christians been killed for their beliefs since 1975?

Stage & Screen — What kind of car was Disney's Love Bug?

Written Word — What, according to Lady Macbeth, would not sweeten her little hand?

Music — Who gave up his seat to the Big Bopper, on the plane that killed him?

Famous People — Nicholas Breakspear is the only Englishman to become what?

Sport & Leisure — In modern fencing, the swords used are the sabre, epée and which other?

Science & Tech — What planet does the moon Ganymede belong to?

True or False? — Mars Bars were created by a Mr Mars; true or false?

ANSWERS: PAGE 91

Food & Drink What substance is the basic ingredient of mead?

 Natural World What is the collective name for a group of badgers?

 History Which English king did Robert the Bruce defeat at Bannockburn?

 Culture & Belief What Christian celebration is Advent a time of preparation for?

 Stage & Screen What was Dirty Harry's surname?

 Written Word Who wrote the *Foundation* trilogy of sci-fi novels?

 Music *The Flowers of the Forest* is a lament for the dead of which battle between England and Scotland?

 Famous People What religion is Richard Gere a follower of?

 Sport & Leisure What was the score in the first ever football international, between Scotland and England?

 Science & Tech What comet is thought to have been seen as the Star of Bethlehem, foretelling the birth of Christ?

True or False? Music to be played at 'allegro tempo' would be played at a very slow speed; true or false?

ANSWERS: PAGE 91

Food & Drink
What is the literal translation of the German dish sauerkraut?

 Natural World
What is the largest mammal in the world?

 History
Who was Britain's last reigning Stuart monarch?

 Culture & Belief
Which of the 12 Apostles is the patron saint of tax officials?

 Stage & Screen
What comedy series' central character is a Seattle-based radio psychiatrist?

 Written Word
Shakespeare's Romeo and Juliet became Tony and Maria in what Broadway smash hit musical?

 Music
Who wrote the musical *Blood Brothers*?

 Famous People
Who was Elizabeth I's mother?

 Sport & Leisure
The St Andrew's Club was founded during the reign of which golf-playing queen?

 Science & Tech
Who was the first woman to fly the Atlantic?

 True or False?
Iceland's President Finnbogadottir, elected in 1980, was the world's first elected female head of state; true or false?

ANSWERS: PAGE 91

Food & Drink
If a Scotsman is eating champit neeps, what is on his plate?

Natural World
Salmon fishing and whisky distilling are associated with a particular Scottish river; what is it?

History
What area was brought under British control by the Opium War?

Culture & Belief
What is the newspaper of the Salvation Army?

Stage & Screen
What classic TV series featured two brothers called Little Joe and Hoss?

Written Word
What is the full name of Major Major in *Catch 22*?

Music
Which unlikely duo paired up on the 1980s' hit *Barcelona*?

Famous People
Which pop star took lead roles in *Ned Kelly*, *Performance* and *Freejack*?

Sport & Leisure
What shape is the field where a baseball match is played?

Science & Tech
On the Mohs hardness scale, what is the hardest mineral?

True or False?
Hong Kong has more skyscrapers than New York; true or false?

ANSWERS: PAGE 92

Food & Drink
How many teaspoons of sugar are there in one packet of jelly?

Natural World
What is Holy Island, off England's north-east coast, also known as?

History
Which type of aeroplanes competed for the Schneider Trophy?

Culture & Belief
Where would you expect to see a Mexican Wave?

Stage & Screen
Who spent years fighting the Autons, Silurians, Sea Devils and Drashigs?

Written Word
In what branch of business are Man Booker Prize sponsors The Man Group?

Music
The Rogers and Hammerstein musical *Carousel* was the source of what famous football anthem?

Famous People
Where was Labour leader John Smith buried?

Sport & Leisure
How many men make up a baseball team?

Science & Tech
Which two stations are connected by the Glasgow to London west coast rail line?

True or False?
The most common surname in both Britain and the USA is Smith; true or false?

ANSWERS: PAGE 92

Food & Drink
If an egg floats on water, is it fresh or stale?

Natural World
Apart from lying down, what can fish not do as they sleep?

History
When was the United Nations charter signed, in San Francisco?

Culture & Belief
What was The Sweeney cockney rhyming slang for?

Stage & Screen
What cult TV detective series saw Bruce Willis first make his name?

Written Word
Where in Aberdeenshire was Robert Louis Stevenson living when he wrote *Treasure Island*?

Music
Who played the role of Jim Morrison in the 1991 film *The Doors*?

Famous People
Which battle was Nelson's last?

Sport & Leisure
What footballing first did Stanley Matthews achieve in 1965?

Science & Tech
What did Charles Lindbergh call his Atlantic-crossing plane?

True or False?
On the *Bounty*, William Bligh actually held the rank of lieutenant; true or false?

ANSWERS: PAGE 92

Food & Drink

Which biscuit is named after an Italian soldier?

 Natural World

What Hebridean island is Fingal's Cave on?

 History

What state saw the last executions for witchcraft in the USA?

 Culture & Belief

What ancient Celtic festival marks the old year's end with a driving away of the spirits of the newly dead?

 Stage & Screen

What instrument does Lisa Simpson play?

 Written Word

Which novelist created the character of lawyer Atticus Finch?

 Music

What band did Frank Sinatra sing with before going solo?

 Famous People

What more light-footed name was Frederick Austerlitz better known as?

 Sport & Leisure

Which two teams have football grounds called the Stadium of Light?

 Science & Tech

Which lightweight metal is made from bauxite?

 True or False?

Sharp-shooter Annie Oakley once shot a cigarette from between the lips of Kaiser Wilhelm; true or false?

ANSWERS: PAGE 92

Food & Drink — What is a Pink Lady?

 Natural World — Which Scottish island is known as 'Scotland in miniature'?

 History — In what battle did Henry V defeat the French in 1415?

 Culture & Belief — In the song, how many presents were handed over on the 12th day of Christmas?

 Stage & Screen — What was the most enduring and coveted creation of MGM art director Cedric Gibbons?

 Written Word — The title of the war novel *Fair Stood the Wind for France* originally referred to what medieval battle?

 Music — Which rock singer/producer wrote the words for the Lloyd Webber musical *Whistle Down the Wind*?

 Famous People — Explorer Henry Stanley fought in the American Civil War. On which side?

 Sport & Leisure — What is the penalty if a show jumper falls off their horse?

 Science & Tech — What chemical element has the atomic number one?

 True or False? — John F. Kennedy features on the back of the US $50 bill; true or false?

ANSWERS: PAGE 92

Food & Drink

When might you eat a simnel cake?

Natural World

Which rivers run through Dublin and Cardiff?

History

Which was the first industry to be nationalized in post-war Britain?

Culture & Belief

What does the phrase 'fiat lux' mean?

Stage & Screen

Martin Shaw, Ben Kingsley and Joanna Lumley all appeared in what long-running TV series?

Written Word

Which cult Scottish author adds a middle initial 'M' to his name on his science fiction novels?

Music

Which little boy did the Coasters sing about, asking *Why's everybody always pickin' on me*??

Famous People

Which modern-day politician once famously declared that there was no such thing as society?

Sport & Leisure

What two winter sports make up the biathlon?

Science & Tech

What is hi-fi abbreviated from?

True or False?

Britain's greatest sailor, Admiral Nelson, suffered terribly from seasickness; true or false?

ANSWERS: PAGE 93

Food & Drink How many minutes of housework are required to burn off the calories in a 25g bag of crisps?

 Natural World The Menai Bridge links mainland Wales and which island?

 History The rationing of what ended on 15 March 1949?

 Culture & Belief How did French economist Proudhon answer his own question 'What is property?'

 Stage & Screen What US comedy show started the careers of stars like Eddie Murphy and Billy Crystal?

 Written Word Author John Buchan became Governor-general of what Commonwealth country?

 Music What Glasgow rock band shares its name with an Austrian Archduke?

 Famous People Newspaper owner and politician Lord Beaverbrook was born in which country?

 Sport & Leisure Who has won the most motor racing World Championships?

 Science & Tech Where in a building would you find headers, stretchers, halfbats and queen closers?

 True or False? A cummerbund is worn around the head; true or false?

ANSWERS: PAGE 93

Food & Drink

In the names of beers, what do the amounts 60 Shilling, 70 Shilling and 80 Shilling represent?

Natural World

Which channel divides Wales from Ireland?

History

What was the name given to Ronald Reagan's economic policies?

Culture & Belief

In Rome, the goddess of wisdom was Minerva. Who was her Greek counterpart?

Stage & Screen

What was Dr Who's Time And Relative Dimensions In Space machine better known as?

Written Word

What was the first thing Kingsley Amis said he would buy with his Booker Prize?

Music

Whose book was called *The One Who Writes the Words for Elton John*?

Famous People

How did cosmonaut Yuri Gagarin die?

Sport & Leisure

Which sport features the Sugar Bowl, Rose Bowl and Cotton Bowl?

Science & Tech

Where might you normally see the Welsh phrase 'Pleidiol wyf im gwlad'?

True or False?

Israel has the largest Jewish population in the world; true or false?

ANSWERS: PAGE 93

Which pudding comes from the root of the cassava plant?

What constellation are the stars Castor and Pollux in?

How long did the first circumnavigation of the earth via the two poles take?

What do Americans call an apartment with two floors?

What cities are home to the Abbey, Citizens and Crucible theatres?

What historic event took place at midnight in the book *Midnight's Children*?

Which number was Schubert's Unfinished Symphony?

What did Howard Carter and the Earl of Carnarvon find in 1922?

What adjective is used to describe Goodwood Racecourse?

In 1962, which train made its centenary journey?

The first powered flight by the Wright brothers lasted for 62 seconds; true or false?

Food & Drink

Sailors combated which disease with limes for vitamin C?

Natural World

The mistral winds blow from which mountains?

History

In 1971 East Pakistan became which independent nation?

Culture & Belief

Where about your person might you find a hologram of William Shakespeare?

Stage & Screen

Liberty Bell was the signature tune for what completely different comedy show in the 1960s?

Written Word

Which Scottish loch is the setting for Sir Walter Scott's *The Lady of the Lake*?

Music

Which singer had the most hits without ever reaching number 1?

Famous People

Who was the American rock star injured in Eddie Cochrane's fatal 1960 car crash?

Sport & Leisure

What is the perfect score in ten-pin bowling?

Science & Tech

How would you describe an iron bucket coated in zinc?

True or False?

The actor Nicholas Cage is the nephew of director Francis Ford Coppola; true or false?

ANSWERS: PAGE 93

Food & Drink
What type of cheese is traditionally associated with Greek salad?

Natural World
Which is furthest north between Alicante, Majorca and Ibiza?

History
Whose affair with Katharine O'Shea led to the end of his political career?

Culture & Belief
How many pounds does the slang term 'a monkey' mean?

Stage & Screen
Which is the odd one out: Snowy, Roobarb and Felix?

Written Word
What TV host said of his *Unreliable Memoirs* 'nothing is factual except the bits that sound like fiction'?

Music
What word described Lips Inc's town, the Goodies' gibbon and Jasper Carrot's moped?

Famous People
Who was the first Tudor king of England?

Sport & Leisure
Bishen Bedi was a spin bowler, taking 266 test wickets for which country?

Science & Tech
What would astonomers measure in parsecs?

True or False?
Edinburgh has the oldest university in Scotland; true or false?

ANSWERS: PAGE 94

Food & Drink
How long does it take for one unit of alcohol to leave the body?

 Natural World
How many stars appear on the state flag of Texas?

 History
Who was elected Richard Nixon's vice-president?

 Culture & Belief
What country features the chrysanthemum on its imperial crest?

 Stage & Screen
What were the wars being fought in *The Green Berets*, *The Blue Max* and *Cross Of Iron*?

 Written Word
Whose poems of obituary in *Private Eye* invariably begin: 'So, farewell then…'?

 Music
Between July 1964 and August 1966, how many consecutive number 1s did the Beatles have?

 Famous People
Who painted *The Monarch of the Glen* and designed the lions in Trafalgar Square?

 Sport & Leisure
The bodyline method of bowling was introduced to combat which Australian?

 Science & Tech
Which Scottish railway station was named after a now-closed sewing machine factory?

 True or False?
Stirling Moss never won the world motor racing championship; true or false?

ANSWERS: PAGE 94

Food & Drink
How much milk does it take to make a pound of cheese?

Natural World
What are the two main metals combined to make bronze?

History
Where did the Americans' abortive invasion of Cuba take place?

Culture & Belief
Until 1836, there were only six universities in Britain: Oxford, Cambridge and which other four?

Stage & Screen
Who originally presented *Juke Box Jury*?

Written Word
Which Shakespeare character says 'But soft! What light through yonder window breaks'?

Music
Who composed the opera *Lakme* and the ballet *Coppelia*?

Famous People
Tony Blair became the fourth post-war Labour prime minister. Who were the other three?

Sport & Leisure
Which cricket side won the first ever County Championship and Sunday League double?

Science & Tech
Which peasant group destroyed machinery which they feared would destroy their livelihood?

True or False?
Ferdinand Magellan was Spanish; true or false?

ANSWERS: PAGE 94

Food & Drink
Which crop is threatened by the Colorado beetle?

Natural World
What is the height of Ben Nevis in metres?

History
What did Captain Robert Jenkins display in London in 1738, leading to a war with Spain?

Culture & Belief
On the Queen's coat of arms, which country is represented by the unicorn?

Stage & Screen
Who was Isabella Rossellini's famous mother?

Written Word
In which three successive years in the 1950s was *Lord of the Rings* published in three parts?

Music
What is a violinist's bow string made of?

Famous People
Which wit declared that 'Nothing succeeds like excess'?

Sport & Leisure
Who, in 1970, was the first Briton for 50 years to win the US Golf Open?

Science & Tech
How would the police catch a criminal using dactylography?

True or False?
Sir Walter Raleigh was responsible for introducing the potato to Britain; true or false?

ANSWERS: PAGE 94

Food & Drink What are Kerr's Pinks and Maris Pipers?

 Natural World If hens sit on their eggs for three weeks, how long do swans sit on theirs?

 History When were British women given equal voting rights to men?

 Culture & Belief Which 13th-century saint's followers were known as the Grey Friars?

 Stage & Screen Which famous dancer directed the film *Hello Dolly*?

 Written Word Which American author has written extensively about everyday life in Lake Wobegon?

 Music What colour is common to hits by Fleetwood Mac, The Lemon Pipers and Shakin' Stevens?

 Famous People Which star of the Kirov ballet defected in 1979?

 Sport & Leisure What sport would you play with a mashie?

 Science & Tech Chuck Yeager was the first pilot to break what?

 True or False? All horses have the same official birthday; true or false?

ANSWERS: PAGE 94

Food & Drink
What useful digestive function do the leaves and pods of the senna plant perform?

Natural World
Which northern Scottish island gave its name to a style of pullover?

History
What were the three estates traditionally seen as making up the medieval kingdom?

Culture & Belief
The Royal Company of Archers serve as the Queen's bodyguard in which country?

Stage & Screen
Which actor appeared as Ivanhoe, The Saint and James Bond?

Written Word
After Bonkers the dog bit Garp's ear, how did Garp get his own back?

Music
Deacon Blue took their name from a track by which band?

Famous People
Derek Hatton was a councillor in which English city?

Sport & Leisure
Royal Blackheath is the oldest what in England?

Science & Tech
Which two architectural orders are combined in the composite order?

True or False?
The term 'Art Deco' came into use in the mid 1920s; true or false?

ANSWERS: PAGE 95

What type of tree is the source of sago?

 Peruvian guano was first used as a fertilizer in the 1840s. What is guano?

 What century saw the end of the Chinese Ming dynasty?

 In Scandinavian mythology whose souls went to Valhalla?

 What film did Charlie Chaplin first speak in?

 What is the subject of Horace McCoy's *They Shoot Horses, Don't They*?

 Who was the bald-headed singer in Classix Nouveau?

 Alfred the Great founded which one of the three modern-day armed services?

 Which team was the first winner of the Scottish Cup in 1874?

 What was made by the Manhattan Project?

 A dowry was originally brought to a marriage by the male partner; true or false?

ANSWERS: PAGE 95

Food & Drink
Which bottled water used the advertising slogan 'L'eau and behold'?

 Natural World
What Scottish region is Gretna Green in?

 History
Which sultanate and empire was known in the 19th and early 20th centuries as the 'sick man of Europe'?

 Culture & Belief
Terence Rattigan dedicated *The Winslow Boy* to which boy who later became one of Mrs Thatcher's cabinet?

 Stage & Screen
When did Superman first appear on TV (to within two years)?

 Written Word
In which year was Orwell's *1984* published?

 Music
Hamlet Cigars' adverts have become identified with which piece of music by J. S. Bach?

 Famous People
Name the city where David Dinkins was the first black mayor.

 Sport & Leisure
Which English football team dropped Woolwich from its name?

 Science & Tech
The first paper hankies, Celluwipes, were given which new name by manufacturers Kimberley-Clark?

 True or False?
Shredded Wheat was the first commercially produced breakfast cereal; true or false?

ANSWERS: PAGE 95

Food & Drink
Which drinks company sponsors the comedy award at the Edinburgh Festival Fringe?

 Natural World
Of stalactites and stalagmites, which grow upwards?

 History
What term was given to the ritual of prostrating oneself before the Chinese emperor?

 Culture & Belief
Which low, stuffed seat with no back is named after the Turkish empire?

 Stage & Screen
Which Hollywood superstar established the Sundance Institute to promote independent movie-making?

 Written Word
Who wrote *Jaws*?

 Music
Who was the long-tongued star of Bad Manners?

 Famous People
Golfer Vijay Singh is a native of which country?

 Sport & Leisure
Who was the last amateur to win the Open golf championship?

 Science & Tech
From which phrase was the word 'radar' extracted?

 True or False?
A Batmitzvah is the female equivalent of a Barmitzvah; true or false?

ANSWERS: PAGE 95

Food & Drink
How do green vegetables differ from root vegetables?

Natural World
Which animal is a cross between a male ass and a female horse?

History
Who was the 'Sea-Green Incorruptible' who led the reign of terror in revolutionary France?

Culture & Belief
What was the difference between a highwayman and a footpad?

Stage & Screen
Which canine star left her prints on the cement outside Mann's Chinese Theater?

Written Word
Who is the Edinburgh detective created by author Ian Rankin?

Music
Who played Che Guevara in the original London cast of *Evita*?

Famous People
Whose gang were the perpetrators of the St Valentine's Day Massacre?

Sport & Leisure
In the 1970s, which horse racing trophy did Sagaro win three times?

Science & Tech
Which institutions benefit from using the Dewey decimal system?

True or False?
The original Greek Olympic Games took place every 10 years; true or false?

ANSWERS: PAGE 95

Which has more calories, a pint of lager, a pint of cider or a can of coke?

 How would a python kill its prey?

 In an essay in 1734, what did Alexander Pope say is the proper study of mankind?

 Waitangi Day is a national holiday in which country?

 What 1942 classic is the most frequently shown film on US TV?

 Which book was selected in 2005 as the best-ever Scottish book?

 Which singer/songwriter sang 'I'll have to say I love you in a song'?

 Who began in *The Sweeney* before graduating to Oxford as *Inspector Morse*?

 What was Ray Reardon's occupation before he became a snooker professional?

 What was the trademark name for the plastic resin developed by Leo Baekeland?

 A 50p piece has seven edges; true or false?

ANSWERS: PAGE 96

Food & Drink
Which cooking ingredient was developed from the Paisley textile trade?

 Natural World
At what age do human males reach half their adult height?

 History
Which car manufacturer made the Anglia?

 Culture & Belief
How were the great plagues of the Middle Ages transmitted?

 Stage & Screen
Who or what was 'Alex' in the title of the film, *Ice Cold In Alex*?

 Written Word
Who wrote *Cat on a Hot Tin Roof*?

 Music
What was the Troggs' only number 1?

 Famous People
What title was held by Irish soldier and statesman Arthur Wellesley?

 Sport & Leisure
Which racecourse hosts the Scottish Grand National?

 Science & Tech
The first example of what device was fitted by Blaupunkt into a Studebaker?

 True or False?
The first car speedometers only went up to 35 mph; true or false?

ANSWERS: PAGE 96

Food & Drink
Which name, from an Italian city, is given to a two- or three-flavoured ice cream?

Natural World
Which island group includes Mallorca, Menorca and Ibiza?

History
Early digital watches featured LED displays. What does LED stand for?

Culture & Belief
Which Greek philosopher was taught by Socrates, and in turn taught Aristotle?

Stage & Screen
What cinematic award was originally nicknamed a Stella?

Written Word
How many lines are in a sonnet?

Music
Which opera features the *Toreador's Song*?

Famous People
Which entertainer insured his distinctive front teeth for £4million?

Sport & Leisure
At what distance was Roger Black British number one?

Science & Tech
Bell made the first long-distance telephone call in 1892 between which two American cities?

True or False?
Jim Clark was the first to win the world motor racing driver's championship posthumously; true or false?

ANSWERS: PAGE 96

Food & Drink
Fray Bentos is a port in which country?

 Natural World
Niagara Falls is between which two Great Lakes?

 History
How many pennies were in an old style British pound?

 Culture & Belief
On a map of the London Underground, which line is coloured grey?

 Stage & Screen
What now regular event took place at Hollywood's Roosevelt Hotel on 16 May 1929?

 Written Word
According to Jeanette Winterson, what are oranges not?

 Music
Johnny Wakelin had two hits with songs about which sportsman?

 Famous People
What was army chaplain Geoffrey Anketell Studdert-Kennedy nicknamed for giving soldiers cigarettes?

 Sport & Leisure
Which British sporting venue includes the Paddock Hill grandstand?

 Science & Tech
What was the innovative feature of the Rolex 'Oyster' watch?

 True or False?
By law, Scotch whisky must be left for five years after distilling before it can be sold; true or false?

ANSWERS: PAGE 96

Food & Drink
What ingredient forms the topping on crème brûlée?

 Natural World
Which Scottish island group features Skara Brae, Scapa Flow and the Old Man of Hoy?

 History
Whose first volume of war memoirs was called *Adolf Hitler: My Part in his Downfall*?

 Culture & Belief
In pantomime, whose sweetheart was Columbine?

 Stage & Screen
How tall, to the nearest inch, is an Oscar statuette?

 Written Word
Who is the salesman in Arthur Miller's *Death of a Salesman*?

 Music
Who wrote the Monkees' hit *I'm a Believer*?

 Famous People
After the Vietnam war, what was the new name for Saigon?

 Sport & Leisure
Donald and Malcolm Campbell both drove vehicles with which name?

 Science & Tech
Which item of office stationery do the French call 'trombones'?

 True or False?
The Smurfs were originally known as Les Schtroumpfs; true or false?

ANSWERS: PAGE 96

THE QUIZ BOOK *ANSWERS*

SET 1

Food & Drink:	A poisoned apple	**Famous People:**	Arthur Miller and
Natural World:	Osprey		Marilyn Monroe
History:	Two	**Sport & Leisure:**	For winning the US
Culture & Belief:	Eros		Masters and leading
Stage & Screen:	Four		the Tour de France
Written Word:	Melchester	**Science & Tech:**	Stephen Hawking
Music:	The road to Mandalay	**True or False?**	True

SET 2

Food & Drink:	Manna	**Famous People:**	Allan Pinkerton
Natural World:	Four inches	**Sport & Leisure:**	Kirkcaldy
History:	Caligula	**Science & Tech:**	Karl Benz
Culture & Belief:	Christian Dior	**True or False?**	True
Stage & Screen:	*Z Cars*		
Written Word:	The Canterbury Tales		
Music:	Beethoven		

SET 3

Food & Drink:	Juniper	**Stage & Screen:**	*North By Northwest*
Natural World:	Chicago	**Written Word:**	John Osborne
History:	To sound less German	**Music:**	Noel Gallagher
	in WWI (it was a	**Famous People:**	Charles Darwin
	name-change)	**Sport & Leisure:**	*Pot Black*
Culture & Belief:	Ecuador (they were	**Science & Tech:**	On the side of a ship
	shipped from Panama)	**True or False?**	True

SET 4

Food & Drink:	A cheese	**Music:**	*Reasons To Be*
Natural World:	The Northern Lights		*Cheerful, Part 3*
History:	None	**Famous People:**	Aviation
Culture & Belief:	The Ten	**Sport & Leisure:**	The Jules Rimet
	Commandments		Trophy
Stage & Screen:	Charlton Heston	**Science & Tech:**	The de Havilland Comet
Written Word:	Erskine Childers	**True or False?**	True (in 1892)

SET 5

Food & Drink:	Smash Instant Mashed	**Written Word:**	Silas Marner
	Potato	**Music:**	A miner 49-er
Natural World:	Aurora australis	**Famous People:**	Work
History:	26	**Sport & Leisure:**	1972
Culture & Belief:	Drink from it	**Science & Tech:**	Dynamite
Stage & Screen:	The nickname of	**True or False?**	False (the Queen has
	India's film industry		no passport)

SET 6

Food & Drink:	Turmeric	**Music:**	Richie Valens and the Big Bopper
Natural World:	The River Nile		
History:	Julius Caesar	**Famous People:**	Wallis Simpson
Culture & Belief:	15th March	**Sport & Leisure:**	100m, 200m, 4x100m relay, long jump
Stage & Screen:	Jacques Cousteau's		
Written Word:	Ophelia	**Science & Tech:**	John Dunlop
		True or False?	False

SET 7

Food & Drink:	Bitter	**Music:**	Flowers In The Rain (by The Move)
Natural World:	The intestines of sheep		
History:	Abraham Lincoln	**Famous People:**	All were assassinated
Culture & Belief:	Demons and goblins	**Sport & Leisure:**	India
Stage & Screen:	Scott, Virgil, Alan, Gordon, John	**Science & Tech:**	The Morris Mini
		True or False?	False (all are types of knot)
Written Word:	Mycroft		

SET 8

Food & Drink:	Haggis	**Music:**	Tennessee
Natural World:	A reindeer	**Famous People:**	All were left handed
History:	1863	**Sport & Leisure:**	35–1
Culture & Belief:	The pope	**Science & Tech:**	Uranus
Stage & Screen:	Fred Astaire and Ginger Rogers	**True or False?**	False (there are 9)
Written Word:	Salome		

SET 9

Food & Drink:	Ham and cheese	**Music:**	Louis Armstrong
Natural World:	A meteor	**Famous People:**	Satchel-mouth
History:	The Library of Alexandria	**Sport & Leisure:**	Kenneth Wolstenholme (at the World Cup Final)
Culture & Belief:	£50	**Science & Tech:**	By being the first woman in space
Stage & Screen:	Toto		
Written Word:	Manchester	**True or False?**	True

SET 10

Food & Drink:	Honey	**Music:**	*Rockin' All Over The World* (by Status Quo)
Natural World:	K2		
History:	The First World War ended	**Famous People:**	Orson Welles
		Sport & Leisure:	Uruguay (in 1930)
Culture & Belief:	Ten	**Science & Tech:**	John Glenn
Stage & Screen:	Fred Astaire	**True or False?**	True
Written Word:	Harry Lime		

SET 11

Food & Drink:	Jerusalem artichokes
Natural World:	Shipping areas
History:	James VI of Scotland and I of England
Culture & Belief:	So be it
Stage & Screen:	Celia Johnson and Trevor Howard
Written Word:	Matt Groening
Music:	The Chieftains
Famous People:	Canterbury Cathedral
Sport & Leisure:	Scrabble
Science & Tech:	Just over 8 minutes
True or False?	True

SET 12

Food & Drink:	Coca-Cola
Natural World:	Canberra
History:	The Confederacy
Culture & Belief:	Hope
Stage & Screen:	*St Elmo's Fire*
Written Word:	Smallville
Music:	A septet
Famous People:	Andrew Carnegie
Sport & Leisure:	Weightlifting
Science & Tech:	DNA
True or False?	False

SET 13

Food & Drink:	A lemon
Natural World:	Greenland
History:	Seven
Culture & Belief:	25th March, year 0
Stage & Screen:	*The White Horses*
Written Word:	George Orwell
Music:	Both had hits with *Amazing Grace*
Famous People:	Václav Havel
Sport & Leisure:	Scotland and England
Science & Tech:	The structure of DNA
True or False?	True

SET 14

Food & Drink:	Whisky (meaning 'water of life')
Natural World:	Poland
History:	The Great Exhibition of 1851
Culture & Belief:	The Mormon church
Stage & Screen:	Weatherfield
Written Word:	George Bernard Shaw
Music:	Harry Lauder
Famous People:	Buzz Aldrin
Sport & Leisure:	Trevor Francis
Science & Tech:	Each was named after its inventor
True or False?	True

SET 15

Food & Drink:	Aubergine
Natural World:	The fast speed of its beating wings
History:	Richard Cromwell
Culture & Belief:	Hinduism
Stage & Screen:	The Archers
Written Word:	Ronald Reagan
Music:	Simon Rattle
Famous People:	Charles Stewart Parnell
Sport & Leisure:	1984 (Los Angeles)
Science & Tech:	Rust
True or False?	False (it is Mandarin)

SET 16

Food & Drink:	Prawns
Natural World:	Istanbul
History:	US troops in Britain in WWII
Culture & Belief:	David
Stage & Screen:	Flipper and Skippy
Written Word:	Gnasher
Music:	Andy Stewart
Famous People:	Oscar Wilde
Sport & Leisure:	Athens (in 1896)
Science & Tech:	Viruses
True or False?	True

SET 17

Food & Drink:	The Greek gods
Natural World:	Nepal
History:	Culloden
Culture & Belief:	Coca-Cola's
Stage & Screen:	Tennessee Williams
Written Word:	A La Recherche Du Temps Perdu
	(by Marcel Proust)
Music:	Blur
Famous People:	Billy Graham
Sport & Leisure:	22
Science & Tech:	32
True or False?	False (it was curry)

SET 18

Food & Drink:	Garibaldi
Natural World:	Everything
History:	Hawaii
Culture & Belief:	One (French)
Stage & Screen:	Father Ted
Written Word:	Walter Scott
Music:	The Gambler
Famous People:	Fidel Castro
Sport & Leisure:	Bjorn Borg
Science & Tech:	$22/7$
True or False?	False (it was a chair-back cover)

SET 19

Food & Drink:	Anna Pavlova
Natural World:	Approx. 3960 miles (6385km)
History:	The prime minister
Culture & Belief:	Woodstock
Stage & Screen:	Mulder and Scully
Written Word:	The Addams Family
Music:	Finger its holes to play notes
Famous People:	Bonnie Prince Charlie
Sport & Leisure:	The Triathlon
Science & Tech:	Surgery
True or False?	False (it was 1914)

SET 20

Food & Drink:	Locusts and wild honey
Natural World:	Fingerprints
History:	Six
Culture & Belief:	St Augustine
Stage & Screen:	Victor Meldrew
Written Word:	Ursula Le Guin
Music:	Babylon Zoo
Famous People:	William Randolph Hearst
Sport & Leisure:	Yachting
Science & Tech:	212 degrees
True or False?	True

SET 21

Food & Drink:	Haggis
Natural World:	Four
History:	Black and blue
Culture & Belief:	Weathermen
Stage & Screen:	Emergency Room
Written Word:	*Lord Of The Flies*
Music:	The Kinks

Famous People:	Che Guevara
Sport & Leisure:	In the USA
Science & Tech:	Too low
True or False?	False (it is a region in Argentina)

SET 22

Food & Drink:	Three years
Natural World:	Lakes
History:	William the Conqueror
Culture & Belief:	To show membership of a club
Stage & Screen:	Hopkirk was a ghost
Written Word:	In Xanadu

Music:	Giacomo Puccini
Famous People:	Boadicea
Sport & Leisure:	2000 Guineas, Derby, St Leger
Science & Tech:	The liver
True or False?	True

SET 23

Food & Drink:	Jonah
Natural World:	Alaska
History:	John F. Kennedy
Culture & Belief:	Saatchi & Saatchi
Stage & Screen:	Fay Wray
Written Word:	It's the temperature books combust at

Music:	Erasure
Famous People:	Gerald Ford
Sport & Leisure:	Pelota
Science & Tech:	273.15
True or False?	True

SET 24

Food & Drink:	Oats
Natural World:	The Angel Falls in Venezuela
History:	Robert Peel
Culture & Belief:	Paper money (it is a wallet)
Stage & Screen:	They are uncle and

	nephew
Written Word:	Mario Puzo
Music:	*The Bells Of Hell*
Famous People:	Lawrence of Arabia
Sport & Leisure:	26 miles 385 yards
Science & Tech:	60 degrees
True or False?	True

SET 25

Food & Drink:	Cow pie
Natural World:	The African elephant
History:	Government Issue
Culture & Belief:	St Swithin
Stage & Screen:	*In Which We Serve*
Written Word:	Brendan Behan
Music:	A solo performance

Famous People:	Vivienne Westwood
Sport & Leisure:	A bamboo sword
Science & Tech:	To prevent them freezing (it is anti-freeze)
True or False?	False (Scotch comes only from Scotland)

SET 26

Food & Drink:	1930s
Natural World:	The Moon's gravitational pull
History:	Shergar
Culture & Belief:	Matthew
Stage & Screen:	*Breakfast At Tiffany's*
Written Word:	The Simpsons
Music:	The Sex Pistols
Famous People:	William Wallace and Robert the Bruce
Sport & Leisure:	30
Science & Tech:	35
True or False?	True

SET 27

Food & Drink:	A Bath Oliver
Natural World:	20 square feet
History:	1801
Culture & Belief:	The Salvation Army
Stage & Screen:	Bill Forsyth
Written Word:	Homer
Music:	*Cats*
Famous People:	Jeremy Bentham
Sport & Leisure:	Boston
Science & Tech:	Four
True or False?	True

SET 28

Food & Drink:	William Pitt the Younger
Natural World:	Three (Scotland, Wales and England)
History:	The *Queen Mary*, the *Queen Elizabeth* and the *QEII*
Culture & Belief:	The mini-skirt
Stage & Screen:	Commander, Royal Navy
Written Word:	James Joyce
Music:	Abba's
Famous People:	Matt Busby
Sport & Leisure:	St Leger
Science & Tech:	Strengthens it
True or False?	False (it was Chicago)

SET 29

Food & Drink:	Curry-flavoured soup
Natural World:	Newly qualified doctors
History:	Pudding Lane
Culture & Belief:	25th March
Stage & Screen:	*Ben Hur, Titanic, The Return of the King*
Written Word:	Sancho Panza
Music:	*My Favourite Things*
Famous People:	Heather Locklear
Sport & Leisure:	Three
Science & Tech:	Hardness
True or False?	True

SET 30

Food & Drink:	Tonic water
Natural World:	The albatross (4m)
History:	H. H. Kitchener
Culture & Belief:	8 days
Stage & Screen:	*Escape To Victory*
Written Word:	*Whisky Galore*
Music:	Vince Hill
Famous People:	Fatty Arbuckle
Sport & Leisure:	Jimmy White
Science & Tech:	Lies
True or False?	False

SET 31

Food & Drink:	The first is Scotch; the other isn't	**Music:**	Keep the red flag flying here
Natural World:	The peregrine (112mph)	**Famous People:**	Phil Spector
History:	The Napoleonic Wars	**Sport & Leisure:**	Gary Sobers
Culture & Belief:	Pentecost	**Science & Tech:**	24
Stage & Screen:	*The Quiet Man*	**True or False?**	False (it was Mr Goodyear)
Written Word:	*Kidnapped & Catriona*		

SET 32

Food & Drink:	432	**Music:**	The book of the performance
Natural World:	Bread	**Famous People:**	Elvis Costello
History:	King Edward I	**Sport & Leisure:**	Korea
Culture & Belief:	1,788	**Science & Tech:**	30 stone
Stage & Screen:	Wimbledon Common	**True or False?**	True
Written Word:	*The Arabian Nights Entertainment*		

SET 33

Food & Drink:	The Earl of Sandwich		Whitney Houston
Natural World:	The North & Baltic Seas	**Famous People:**	Adolf Hitler
History:	It was stolen from Westminster Abbey	**Sport & Leisure:**	French & Australian championships, US Open, Wimbledon
Culture & Belief:	Red		
Stage & Screen:	*Rear Window*	**Science & Tech:**	In the air
Written Word:	Knitting	**True or False?**	True
Music:	Dolly Parton and		

SET 34

Food & Drink:	Pancakes	**Music:**	Bill Clinton
Natural World:	The Mariana Trench	**Famous People:**	The Duke of York
History:	The eighth century	**Sport & Leisure:**	Curling
Culture & Belief:	A fresco	**Science & Tech:**	A rainbow
Stage & Screen:	He is assistant to the senior electrician	**True or False?**	False (it is a type of lake)
Written Word:	Banquo's		

SET 35

Food & Drink:	Rum	**Written Word:**	Quasimodo
Natural World:	Off Australia's north-east coast	**Music:**	Bob Dylan
		Famous People:	Victoria
History:	The Community Charge	**Sport & Leisure:**	Wrestling
		Science & Tech:	Cancers in the human body
Culture & Belief:	Art Deco		
Stage & Screen:	*The Terminator*	**True or False?**	True

SET 36

Food & Drink:	Changed water into wine	**Written Word:**	The Drones
Natural World:	46	**Music:**	The exciseman
History:	Edward Heath	**Famous People:**	The Morris Mini
Culture & Belief:	Diapers	**Sport & Leisure:**	15
Stage & Screen:	*Creature Comforts, A Close Shave, the Wrong Trousers*	**Science & Tech:**	Halley's Comet
		True or False?	False (it was the Morris Minor)

SET 37

Food & Drink:	Veal	**Music:**	Johann Strauss I and II
Natural World:	Hippopotamus	**Famous People:**	Fitzgerald
History:	They were father and daughter	**Sport & Leisure:**	12th dan
Culture & Belief:	Stirling	**Science & Tech:**	Apollo 10 (at 39,897kph)
Stage & Screen:	Richard Chamberlain	**True or False?**	False (it is the biggest)
Written Word:	*The Gulag Archipelago*		

SET 38

Food & Drink:	Tea leaves	**Music:**	*Hoots Mon*
Natural World:	Carboniferous	**Famous People:**	The Duke of York
History:	Beefeaters	**Sport & Leisure:**	Kenny Dalglish
Culture & Belief:	A tent-maker	**Science & Tech:**	Apollo 11
Stage & Screen:	Larry Hagman	**True or False?**	False
Written Word:	By setting all the action in *Ulysses* on that day		

SET 39

Food & Drink:	Green		*Belgrano*
Natural World:	It performs no function	**Music:**	A young cowboy all wrapped in white linen
History:	The Liberals		
Culture & Belief:	Jacob	**Famous People:**	Geoffrey Howe
Stage & Screen:	*The Waltons*	**Sport & Leisure:**	Shinty
Written Word:	The sinking of the Argentinian battleship	**Science & Tech:**	Ozone
		True or False?	True (on 14th Jan. 1878)

SET 40

Food & Drink:	Vodka	**Music:**	Detroit, Michigan
Natural World:	Loch Lomond	**Famous People:**	To mark the death of Henry Royce
History:	The pilots who fought the Battle of Britain	**Sport & Leisure:**	The European Champion Clubs' Cup
Culture & Belief:	Confucius		
Stage & Screen:	Ringo Starr	**Science & Tech:**	Cats' eyes
Written Word:	John Knox	**True or False?**	True

SET 41

Food & Drink:	It is start of the grouse-shooting season
Natural World:	3 (Bloemfontein, Cape Town, Pretoria)
History:	Finland
Culture & Belief:	St George, St Andrew, St Patrick
Stage & Screen:	Bill and Ben
Written Word:	The Reichenbach Falls
Music:	Eric Idle
Famous People:	Guy Gibson
Sport & Leisure:	Munro-bagging (climbing mountains over 3000ft)
Science & Tech:	On a church (they are parts of the building)
True or False?	False

SET 42

Food & Drink:	A waiter (it is a tip)
Natural World:	Highland Region
History:	Mexico
Culture & Belief:	The infectious diarrhoea suffered by tourists in Mexico
Stage & Screen:	John Belushi & Dan Aykroyd
Written Word:	Adolf Hitler
Music:	Will Powers
Famous People:	Jean Shrimpton
Sport & Leisure:	Gareth Southgate
Science & Tech:	20
True or False?	False (it is a set of bells hung in a tower)

SET 43

Food & Drink:	Ten
Natural World:	Both male and female
History:	Buttons at the cuff
Culture & Belief:	St Paul's
Stage & Screen:	$250,000
Written Word:	Sherlock Holmes
Music:	Maurice (by one hour)
Famous People:	The Nation of Islam
Sport & Leisure:	Elephant
Science & Tech:	Red, yellow, blue
True or False?	False

SET 44

Food & Drink:	Soup
Natural World:	The iris
History:	24
Culture & Belief:	Good of themselves
Stage & Screen:	*The Third Man*
Written Word:	A troll
Music:	A wooden chair
Famous People:	William Randolph Hearst
Sport & Leisure:	One
Science & Tech:	365ft
True or False?	False

SET 45

Food & Drink:	Mayonnaise
Natural World:	Lion and tiger
History:	10
Culture & Belief:	Love
Stage & Screen:	Honor Blackman
Written Word:	Christoper Robin
Music:	Eternal
Famous People:	Aubrey Beardsley
Sport & Leisure:	Rangers
Science & Tech:	Cantilever
True or False?	True

SET 46

Food & Drink:	Green
Natural World:	The Shetland Islands
History:	The NHS
Culture & Belief:	The crucifixion of Christ
Stage & Screen:	Ron Moody
Written Word:	Leslie Halliwell

Music:	Mike McGear
Famous People:	Michael Fagin
Sport & Leisure:	Canada
Science & Tech:	Harris tweed
True or False?	False (it is the Falabella)

SET 47

Food & Drink:	Bicarbonate of soda
Natural World:	32
History:	It brought the first West Indian immigrants
Culture & Belief:	Easter
Stage & Screen:	Toothpaste
Written Word:	Long John Silver

Music:	The Scaffold
Famous People:	Samoa
Sport & Leisure:	1968
Science & Tech:	Four
True or False?	True

SET 48

Food & Drink:	Atlanta, Georgia
Natural World:	The Canaries
History:	Macbeth
Culture & Belief:	East Timor
Stage & Screen:	A Volkswagen Beetle
Written Word:	All the perfumes of Arabia

Music:	Waylon Jennings
Famous People:	Pope
Sport & Leisure:	Foil
Science & Tech:	Jupiter
True or False?	True

SET 49

Food & Drink:	Honey
Natural World:	A cete
History:	Edward II
Culture & Belief:	Christmas
Stage & Screen:	Callahan
Written Word:	Isaac Asimov
Music:	Flodden

Famous People:	Buddhism
Sport & Leisure:	0-0
Science & Tech:	Halley's Comet
True or False?	False (it would be quick and lively)

SET 50

Food & Drink:	Sour cabbage
Natural World:	The blue whale
History:	Queen Anne
Culture & Belief:	Matthew
Stage & Screen:	*Frasier*
Written Word:	*West Side Story*
Music:	Willy Russell

Famous People:	Anne Boleyn
Sport & Leisure:	Mary, Queen of Scots
Science & Tech:	Amelia Earhart
True or False?	True

SET 51

Food & Drink:	Mashed turnip
Natural World:	The Spey
History:	Hong Kong
Culture & Belief:	*The War Cry*
Stage & Screen:	*Bonanza*
Written Word:	Major Major Major Major

Music:	Freddie Mercury, Monserrat Caballe
Famous People:	Mick Jagger
Sport & Leisure:	Diamond
Science & Tech:	Diamond
True or False?	False

SET 52

Food & Drink:	19
Natural World:	Lindisfarne
History:	Seaplanes
Culture & Belief:	In a grandstand
Stage & Screen:	Dr Who
Written Word:	Broking
Music:	*You'll Never Walk Alone*

Famous People:	Iona
Sport & Leisure:	Nine
Science & Tech:	Glasgow Central and London Euston
True or False?	True

SET 53

Food & Drink:	Stale
Natural World:	Close their eyes
History:	1945
Culture & Belief:	Flying Squad (Sweeney Todd)
Stage & Screen:	*Moonlighting*
Written Word:	Braemar

Music:	Val Kilmer
Famous People:	Trafalgar
Sport & Leisure:	He was the first footballer to be knighted
Science & Tech:	*The Spirit of St Louis*
True or False?	True

SET 54

Food & Drink:	Garibaldi
Natural World:	Staffa
History:	Massachusetts
Culture & Belief:	Hallowe'en
Stage & Screen:	Saxophone
Written Word:	Harper Lee

Music:	The Tommy Dorsey Band
Famous People:	Fred Astaire
Sport & Leisure:	Sporting Lisbon and Sunderland
Science & Tech:	Aluminium
True or False?	True

SET 55

Food & Drink:	An alcoholic cocktail or an apple
Natural World:	Arran
History:	Agincourt
Culture & Belief:	78
Stage & Screen:	The Oscar statuette
Written Word:	Agincourt

Music:	Jim Steinman
Famous People:	Confederates
Sport & Leisure:	8 points
Science & Tech:	Hydrogen
True or False?	False (he is not on any)

SET 56

Food & Drink:	Easter, Christmas or Mothering Sunday
Natural World:	Liffey and Taff
History:	Coal
Culture & Belief:	Let there be light
Stage & Screen:	*Coronation Street*
Written Word:	Iain Banks
Music:	Charlie Brown
Famous People:	Margaret Thatcher
Sport & Leisure:	Ski-ing and rifle-shooting
Science & Tech:	High fidelity
True or False?	True

SET 57

Food & Drink:	60
Natural World:	Anglesey
History:	Clothing
Culture & Belief:	'Property is theft' –
Stage & Screen:	*Saturday Night Live*
Written Word:	Canada
Music:	Franz Ferdinand
Famous People:	Canada
Sport & Leisure:	Juan Fangio
Science & Tech:	In a brick wall
True or False?	False (it goes around the waist)

SET 58

Food & Drink:	Tax levied on a barrel
Natural World:	St George's Channel
History:	Reaganomics
Culture & Belief:	Athene
Stage & Screen:	The TARDIS
Written Word:	Booze
Music:	Bernie Taupin
Famous People:	In an air crash
Sport & Leisure:	American football
Science & Tech:	On a £1 coin
True or False?	False (it is the USA)

SET 59

Food & Drink:	Tapioca
Natural World:	Gemini
History:	Almost 3 years (2 years 361 days)
Culture & Belief:	Duplex
Stage & Screen:	Dublin, Glasgow and Sheffield
Written Word:	India gained its independence
Music:	Number 8
Famous People:	Tutankhamun's tomb
Sport & Leisure:	Glorious
Science & Tech:	*The Flying Scotsman*
True or False?	False (it was 12 seconds)

SET 60

Food & Drink:	Scurvy
Natural World:	The Alps
History:	Bangladesh
Culture & Belief:	On a cheque card
Stage & Screen:	*Monty Python's Flying Circus*
Written Word:	Loch Katrine
Music:	Nat 'King' Cole
Famous People:	Gene Vincent
Sport & Leisure:	300
Science & Tech:	Galvanised
True or False?	True

SET 61

Food & Drink:	Feta
Natural World:	Majorca
History:	Charles Stewart Parnell
Culture & Belief:	£500
Stage & Screen:	Felix (a cat; the others are dogs)
Written Word:	Clive James
Music:	Funky
Famous People:	Henry VIII
Sport & Leisure:	India
Science & Tech:	Distance
True or False?	False (it is St Andrew's)

SET 62

Food & Drink:	One hour
Natural World:	One
History:	Spiro Agnew
Culture & Belief:	Japan
Stage & Screen:	Vietnam, the First World War and the Second World War
Written Word:	E. J. Thribbs
Music:	Seven
Famous People:	Sir Edwin Landseer
Sport & Leisure:	Don Bradman
Science & Tech:	Singer
True or False?	True

SET 63

Food & Drink:	A gallon
Natural World:	Copper and tin
History:	The Bay of Pigs
Culture & Belief:	St Andrews, Glasgow, Aberdeen, Edinburgh
Stage & Screen:	David Jacobs
Written Word:	Romeo
Music:	Delibes
Famous People:	Attlee, Wilson and Callaghan
Sport & Leisure:	Essex
Science & Tech:	Luddites
True or False?	False (Portuguese)

SET 64

Food & Drink:	Potato
Natural World:	1,344 metres
History:	His severed ear
Culture & Belief:	Scotland
Stage & Screen:	Ingrid Bergman
Written Word:	1954/55/56
Music:	Horsehair
Famous People:	Oscar Wilde
Sport & Leisure:	Tony Jacklin
Science & Tech:	By matching fingerprints
True or False?	True

SET 65

Food & Drink:	Potatoes
Natural World:	Six weeks
History:	1938
Culture & Belief:	St Francis of Assisi
Stage & Screen:	Gene Kelly
Written Word:	Garrison Keillor
Music:	Green (manalishi/ tambourine/door)
Famous People:	Natalia Markova
Sport & Leisure:	Golf (it's a type of club)
Science & Tech:	The sound barrier
True or False?	True (1 January)

SET 66

Food & Drink: They're used as a laxative
Natural World: The Fair Isle
History: Clergy, nobility, commoners
Culture & Belief: Scotland
Stage & Screen: Roger Moore

Written Word: He bit off the dog's ear
Music: Steely Dan
Famous People: Liverpool
Sport & Leisure: Golf club
Science & Tech: Ionic and Corinthian
True or False? False (it wasn't coined until 1966)

SET 67

Food & Drink: Palm tree
Natural World: Bird droppings
History: 17th
Culture & Belief: Heroes killed in battle
Stage & Screen: *The Great Dictator*
Written Word: A dance marathon
Music: Sal Solo

Famous People: The Royal Navy
Sport & Leisure: Queen's Park
Science & Tech: The first atomic bomb
True or False? True

SET 68

Food & Drink: Perrier
Natural World: Dumfries and Galloway
History: Turkey
Culture & Belief: Paul Channon
Stage & Screen: 1956
Written Word: 1949
Music: *Air on a G String*

Famous People: New York
Sport & Leisure: Arsenal
Science & Tech: Kleenex
True or False? True

SET 69

Food & Drink: Perrier
Natural World: Stalagmites
History: Kowtow
Culture & Belief: Ottoman
Stage & Screen: Robert Redford
Written Word: Peter Benchley
Music: Buster Bloodvessel

Famous People: Fiji
Sport & Leisure: Bobby Jones
Science & Tech: ra(dio) d(etecting) a(nd) r(anging)
True or False? True

SET 70

Food & Drink: They grow above the ground
Natural World: A mule
History: Robespierre
Culture & Belief: The highwayman had a horse
Stage & Screen: Lassie

Written Word: Inspector John Rebus
Music: David Essex
Famous People: Al Capone's
Sport & Leisure: The Ascot Gold Cup
Science & Tech: Libraries
True or False? False (every four)

SET 71

Food & Drink:	A can of coke	**Music:**	Jim Croce
Natural World:	By crushing	**Famous People:**	John Thaw
History:	Man	**Sport & Leisure:**	Policeman
Culture & Belief:	New Zealand	**Science & Tech:**	Bakelite
Stage & Screen:	*Casablanca*	**True or False?**	True
Written Word:	*Sunset Song* by Lewis Grassic Gibbon		

SET 72

Food & Drink:	Bisto	**Famous People:**	Duke of Wellington
Natural World:	About two years	**Sport & Leisure:**	Ayr
History:	Ford	**Science & Tech:**	A car radio
Culture & Belief:	By flea bite	**True or False?**	True
Stage & Screen:	The city of Alexandria		
Written Word:	Tennessee Williams		
Music:	*With a Girl Like You*		

SET 73

Food & Drink:	Neapolitan	**Famous People:**	Ken Dodd
Natural World:	The Balearics	**Sport & Leisure:**	400m
History:	Light emitting diode	**Science & Tech:**	New York and Chicago
Culture & Belief:	Plato	**True or False?**	False (it was Jochan Rindt)
Stage & Screen:	BAFTA		
Written Word:	14		
Music:	*Carmen*		

SET 74

Food & Drink:	Uruguay	**Written Word:**	The only fruit
Natural World:	Ontario and Erie	**Music:**	Muhammad Ali
History:	240	**Famous People:**	Woodbine Willie
Culture & Belief:	Jubilee	**Sport & Leisure:**	Brands Hatch
Stage & Screen:	The first Academy Awards (Oscars awards ceremony)	**Science & Tech:**	It was waterproof
		True or False?	False (it's three years)

SET 75

Food & Drink:	Sugar (caramelised)	**Famous People:**	Ho Chi Minh City
Natural World:	Orkney	**Sport & Leisure:**	*Bluebird*
History:	Spike Milligan	**Science & Tech:**	Paper clips
Culture & Belief:	Harlequin	**True or False?**	True
Stage & Screen:	13$\frac{1}{2}$ in (34cm)		
Written Word:	Willy Loman		
Music:	Neil Diamond		